The
HANGRY
Cookbook

Publications International, Ltd.

Photograph on front cover and page 45 copyright © Shutterstock.com.

Pictured on the front cover: Cheesy Tot-Chos *(page 44)*.

Pictured on the back cover *(clockwise from top left):* Raspberry Smoothie
(page 98), Chicken Bacon Quesadillas *(page 25)*, Ramen Joy *(page 116)* and
Jalapeño Poppers *(page 38)*.

ISBN: 978-1-63938-423-5

Manufactured in China.

8 7 6 5 4 3 2 1

Microwave Cooking: Microwave ovens vary in wattage. Use the cooking times
as guidelines and check for doneness before adding more time.

Let's get social!
 @Publications_International
@PublicationsInternational
www.pilbooks.com

CONTENTS

SCOOPABLE SNACKS

PARMESAN RANCH SNACK MIX

Makes about 9½ cups

3 cups corn or rice cereal squares

2 cups oyster crackers

1 package (5 ounces) bagel chips, broken in half

1½ cups mini pretzel twists

1 cup shelled pistachio nuts

2 tablespoons grated Parmesan cheese

¼ cup (½ stick) butter, melted

1 package (1 ounce) dry ranch salad dressing mix

½ teaspoon garlic powder

• •

SLOW COOKER DIRECTIONS

1 Combine cereal, oyster crackers, bagel chips, pretzels, pistachios and cheese in slow cooker; mix gently.

2 Combine butter, salad dressing mix and garlic powder in small bowl. Pour over cereal mixture; toss lightly to coat. Cover; cook on LOW 3 hours.

3 Remove cover; stir gently. Cook, uncovered, on LOW 30 minutes. Serve immediately or cool completely and store in airtight container.

GARLIC-PARMESAN POPCORN

Makes 12 cups

1 tablespoon butter, melted

1 tablespoon olive oil

1 clove garlic, finely minced

12 cups popped popcorn*

⅓ cup grated Parmesan cheese

½ teaspoon dried basil

½ teaspoon dried oregano

Use air-popped popcorn or one bag of microwave popcorn, popped according to package directions.

1 Melt butter in small saucepan over low heat. Stir in oil and garlic.

2 Place popcorn in large bowl; drizzle with butter mixture and toss to coat. Sprinkle with cheese, basil and oregano; toss to coat.

TIP

One regular-size package of microwavable popcorn yields about 10 to 12 cups of popped popcorn.

CRUNCHY RAMEN CHOW

Makes about 8 cups

4 packages (3 ounces each) ramen noodles*

1 cup semisweet chocolate chips

1 cup butterscotch chips

¾ cup creamy peanut butter

¼ cup (½ stick) butter

1½ cups powdered sugar

Use any flavor; discard seasoning packets.

1 Line large baking sheet with waxed or parchment paper. Break noodles into bite-size pieces; place in large bowl.

2 Combine chocolate chips, butterscotch chips, peanut butter and butter in medium microwavable bowl. Microwave on HIGH 1 minute; stir. Continue to heat and stir at 30-second intervals until mixture is melted and smooth.

3 Pour chocolate mixture over noodles; stir to coat evenly.

4 Place powdered sugar in large resealable food storage bag. Add noodle mixture; shake until well coated. Spread in single layer on prepared baking sheet; let stand until set. Store in airtight container.

ROSEMARY NUT MIX

Makes 4 cups

2 tablespoons butter

2 cups pecan halves

1 cup macadamia nuts

1 cup walnuts

1 teaspoon dried rosemary

½ teaspoon salt

¼ teaspoon red pepper flakes

1 Preheat oven to 300°F.

2 Melt butter in large saucepan over low heat. Stir in pecans, macadamia nuts and walnuts. Add rosemary, salt and red pepper flakes; cook and stir 1 minute. Spread mixture on ungreased baking sheet.

3 Bake 8 to 10 minutes or until nuts are fragrant and lightly browned, stirring occasionally. Cool completely on baking sheet on wire rack or serve warm.

POPCORN GRANOLA

Makes 8 servings

1 cup quick oats

6 cups popped popcorn

1 cup golden raisins

½ cup chopped mixed dried fruit

¼ cup sunflower kernels

2 tablespoons butter

2 tablespoons packed brown sugar

1 tablespoon honey

½ teaspoon salt

¼ teaspoon ground cinnamon

¼ teaspoon ground nutmeg

1 Preheat oven to 350°F. Spread oats on ungreased baking sheet; bake 10 to 15 minutes or until lightly toasted, stirring occasionally.

2 Combine oats, popcorn, raisins, dried fruit and sunflower kernels in large bowl.

3 Heat butter, brown sugar, honey, salt, cinnamon and nutmeg in small saucepan over medium heat until butter is melted. Drizzle over popcorn mixture; toss to coat.

CRANBERRY-PRETZEL GORP

Makes about 5 cups

¼ cup (½ stick) butter

¼ cup packed brown sugar

1 tablespoon maple syrup

1 teaspoon curry powder

½ teaspoon ground cinnamon

1½ cups dried cranberries

1½ cups coarsely chopped walnuts and/or slivered almonds

1½ cups salted pretzel nuggets

1 Preheat oven to 300°F. Lightly grease large baking sheet.

2 Combine butter, brown sugar and maple syrup in large saucepan; cook and stir over medium heat until butter is melted and mixture is smooth. Stir in curry powder and cinnamon. Add cranberries, walnuts and pretzels; stir until evenly coated.

3 Spread mixture on prepared pan. Bake 15 minutes or until lightly browned. Cool completely on baking sheet. Store in airtight container.

PARTY POPCORN

Makes 6 quarts

¼ cup vegetable oil

½ cup unpopped popcorn
    kernels

1 teaspoon fine sea salt
    or popcorn salt

4 ounces almond bark,*
    chopped

Rainbow nonpareils

*You can find almond bark by the
chocolate chips in the baking aisle
of the grocery store.*

1 Line two baking sheets with parchment paper.

2 Heat oil in large saucepan over medium-high heat 1 minute.
    Add popcorn; cover with lid and cook 2 to 3 minutes or
    until popcorn slows to about 1 second between pops,
    carefully shaking pan occasionally.

3 Spread popcorn on prepared baking sheets; immediately
    sprinkle with salt and toss gently to blend.

4 Melt almond bark according to package directions. Drizzle
    over popcorn; sprinkle with nonpareils. Let stand until set.

CHOCO-PEANUT BUTTER POPCORN

Makes 6 servings

²/₃ cup semisweet chocolate chips

6 tablespoons creamy peanut butter

2 tablespoons butter

8 cups popped popcorn

½ cup powdered sugar

1 Line baking sheet with waxed or parchment paper. Microwave chocolate chips, peanut butter and butter in medium microwavable bowl on HIGH 30 seconds; stir. Microwave 30 seconds or until melted and smooth. Continue to heat and stir at 30-second intervals until mixture is melted and smooth.

2 Place popcorn in large bowl; pour chocolate mixture over popcorn and stir to coat evenly.

3 Place powdered sugar in large resealable food storage bag. Add popcorn mixture; shake until well coated.

4 Spread in single layer on prepared baking sheet; let stand until set. Store in airtight container.

CRUNCHY FRUITY SNACK MIX

Makes 4 cups

1 cup roasted and salted soy nuts, peanuts or mixed nuts

1 cup pretzel stick halves

²/₃ cup dried cranberries

²/₃ cup dried pineapple, cut into ½-inch pieces

²/₃ cup white chocolate chips

Combine soy nuts, pretzels, cranberries, pineapple and white chocolate chips in large bowl; mix well. Store in airtight container.

CHILI CASHEWS

Makes 2 cups

1 tablespoon vegetable oil

2 teaspoons chili powder

1 teaspoon ground cumin

½ teaspoon sugar

½ teaspoon red pepper flakes

2 cups roasted salted whole cashews

● ● ● ● ● ● ● ● ● ● ● ● ● ● ● ● ● ● ● ●

1 Preheat oven to 350°F. Line baking sheet with foil; spray foil with nonstick cooking spray.

2 Combine oil, chili powder, cumin, sugar and red pepper flakes in medium bowl; stir until well blended. Add cashews, stirring to coat evenly. Spread mixture in single layer on prepared baking sheet.

3 Bake 8 to 10 minutes or until golden, stirring once. Serve warm or cool completely on baking sheet.

STUFFED STUFF

CHICKEN BACON QUESADILLAS

Makes 4 servings

4 teaspoons vegetable oil, divided

4 (8-inch) flour tortillas

1 cup (4 ounces) shredded Colby-Jack cheese

2 cups coarsely chopped cooked chicken

4 slices bacon, crisp-cooked and coarsely chopped

½ cup pico de gallo, plus additional for serving

Sour cream and guacamole (optional)

1 Heat large nonstick skillet over medium heat; brush with 1 teaspoon oil. Place one tortilla in skillet; sprinkle with ¼ cup cheese. Spread ½ cup chicken over one half of tortilla; top with one fourth of bacon and 2 tablespoons pico de gallo.

2 Cook 1 to 2 minutes or until cheese is melted and bottom of tortilla is lightly browned. Fold tortilla over filling, pressing with spatula. Remove to cutting board; cool slightly. Cut into wedges. Repeat with remaining ingredients. Serve with additional pico de gallo, sour cream and guacamole, if desired.

PEPPERONI PEPPER PIZZA POPPERS

Makes 12 pieces

6 mini sweet bell peppers

½ cup marinara or pizza sauce

½ cup (2 ounces) shredded mozzarella cheese

1 teaspoon dried oregano

Optional toppings: sliced olives, sliced mushrooms and/or mini pepperoni slices

1 Preheat oven to 325°F.

2 Slice peppers in half horizontally, removing seeds, but keeping stem intact.

3 Spread sauce in pepper halves. Top with cheese and desired toppings; sprinkle with oregano.

4 Bake 8 to 10 minutes or until cheese is melted and begins to brown.

PEPPERONI BREAD

Makes about 6 servings

1 package (about 14 ounces) refrigerated pizza dough

8 slices provolone cheese

20 to 30 slices pepperoni (about half of 6-ounce package)

½ teaspoon Italian seasoning

¾ cup (3 ounces) shredded mozzarella cheese

½ cup grated Parmesan cheese

1 egg, beaten

Marinara sauce, heated

~~~~~~~~~~~~~~~~~~~~~~~~~~~~~~~

1 Preheat oven to 400°F. Unroll pizza dough on sheet of parchment paper with long side facing you.

2 Arrange half of provolone slices over bottom half of dough, cutting to fit as necessary. Top with pepperoni; sprinkle with ¼ teaspoon Italian seasoning. Top with mozzarella, Parmesan and remaining provolone slices; sprinkle with remaining ¼ teaspoon Italian seasoning.

3 Fold top half of dough over filling; press edges with fork or pinch edges to seal. Slide filled bread on parchment onto large baking sheet. Brush with beaten egg.

4 Bake about 15 minutes or until crust is golden brown. Remove to wire rack to cool slightly. Cut crosswise into slices; serve with marinara sauce.

SPANIKOPITA CUPS

Makes 16 cups

6 tablespoons (¾ stick) butter, melted

2 eggs

1 container (15 ounces) ricotta cheese

1 package (10 ounces) frozen chopped spinach, thawed and squeezed dry

1 package (4 ounces) crumbled feta cheese

¾ teaspoon grated lemon peel

½ teaspoon salt

¼ teaspoon black pepper

⅛ teaspoon ground nutmeg

8 sheets frozen phyllo dough, thawed

1 Preheat oven to 350°F. Brush some of butter into 16 standard (2½-inch) muffin cups.

2 Whisk eggs in large bowl. Add ricotta, spinach, feta, lemon peel, salt, pepper and nutmeg; stir until well blended.

3 Place one sheet of phyllo on work surface. Brush with some of butter; top with second sheet. Repeat with two additional sheets of phyllo. Cut stack of phyllo into eight rectangles; fit rectangles into prepared muffin cups, pressing into bottoms and up sides of cups. Repeat with remaining four sheets of phyllo and butter. Fill phyllo cups evenly with spinach mixture.

4 Bake about 18 minutes or until phyllo is golden brown and filling is set. Cool in pans 2 minutes; remove to wire racks. Serve warm.

QUICK WAFFLED QUESADILLAS

Makes 1 serving

- 2 (6-inch) flour tortillas
- ⅓ cup shredded Cheddar cheese or Monterey Jack cheese
- ¼ cup finely chopped poblano pepper or jalapeño pepper
- 1 small plum tomato, chopped
- ⅛ teaspoon ground cumin
- Salt and black pepper
- ½ ripe medium avocado, chopped
- 1 to 2 tablespoons chopped fresh cilantro
- Juice of ½ lime

1 Preheat classic waffle maker to medium. Coat both sides of each tortilla with nonstick cooking spray.

2 Top one tortilla with cheese, poblano pepper, tomato and cumin; season with salt and black pepper. Top with other tortilla. Place on waffle maker; close, pressing down slightly. Cook 3 minutes or until golden brown and cheese is melted.

3 Cut quesadilla into quarters; serve with avocado, cilantro and lime juice.

TIP

If cheese runs over, let the waffle maker cool completely—the cheese will harden and be easy to remove.

MICRO MINI STUFFED POTATOES

Makes 4 servings

1 pound small new red potatoes

¼ cup sour cream

2 tablespoons butter, softened

½ teaspoon minced garlic

¼ cup milk

½ cup (2 ounces) shredded sharp Cheddar cheese

½ teaspoon salt

¼ teaspoon black pepper

¼ cup finely chopped green onions (optional)

1 Pierce potatoes with fork in several places. Microwave potatoes on HIGH 5 to 6 minutes or until tender. Let stand 5 minutes; cut in half lengthwise. Scoop out pulp from potatoes; set potato shells aside.

2 Combine potato pulp, sour cream, butter and garlic in medium bowl; mix well. Add milk; stir until smooth. Add cheese, salt and pepper; stir until blended.

3 Fill potato shells evenly with potato mixture. Place on plate. Microwave on HIGH 1 to 2 minutes or until cheese melts. Garnish with green onions.

MINI SAUSAGE AND KALE DEEP-DISH PIZZAS

Makes 12 pizzas

1 tablespoon olive oil

4 ounces spicy turkey or pork Italian sausage

1/3 cup finely chopped red onion

2 1/2 cups packed chopped stemmed kale

1/4 teaspoon salt

1 pound refrigerated pizza dough

3/4 cup (3 ounces) shredded Italian cheese blend

1/4 cup pizza sauce

1 Preheat oven to 400°F. Spray 12 standard (2½-inch) muffin cups with nonstick cooking spray.

2 Heat oil in large skillet over medium-high heat. Remove sausage from casings; crumble into skillet. Cook and stir about 5 minutes or until no longer pink. Transfer to plate. Add onion to skillet; cook and stir 4 minutes or until softened. Add kale; cook about 10 minutes or until tender, stirring occasionally. Return sausage to skillet with salt; mix well.

3 Divide dough into 12 pieces. Stretch or roll each piece into 5-inch circle; press into prepared muffin cups. Sprinkle 1 teaspoon cheese into bottom of each cup; spread 1 teaspoon pizza sauce over cheese. Top evenly with kale mixture and remaining cheese.

4 Bake about 15 minutes or until golden brown. Cool in pan 1 minute; loosen sides with small spatula or knife. Remove to wire rack. Serve warm.

JALAPEÑO POPPERS

Makes 24 poppers

12 fresh jalapeño peppers

1 package (8 ounces) cream cheese, softened

1½ cups (6 ounces) shredded Cheddar cheese, divided

2 green onions, finely chopped

½ teaspoon onion powder

¼ teaspoon salt

⅛ teaspoon garlic powder

6 slices bacon, crisp-cooked and finely chopped

2 tablespoons panko or plain dry bread crumbs

2 tablespoons grated Parmesan or Romano cheese

1 Preheat oven to 375°F. Line baking sheet with parchment paper or foil.

2 Cut each jalapeño pepper in half lengthwise; remove ribs and seeds.

3 Combine cream cheese, 1 cup Cheddar cheese, green onions, onion powder, salt and garlic powder in medium bowl. Stir in bacon. Fill each jalapeño pepper half with about 1 tablespoon cheese mixture. Place on prepared baking sheet. Sprinkle with remaining ½ cup Cheddar cheese, panko, if desired, and Parmesan cheese.

4 Bake 10 to 12 minutes or until cheeses are melted and jalapeño peppers are slightly softened.

CHOCOLATE STUFFED DOUGHNUTS

Makes 10 doughnuts

½ cup semisweet chocolate chips

2 tablespoons whipping cream

1 package (7½ ounces) refrigerated buttermilk biscuits (10 biscuits)

½ cup granulated or powdered sugar

¾ cup vegetable oil

1 Combine chocolate chips and cream in small microwavable bowl. Microwave on HIGH 20 seconds; stir until smooth. Heat and stir at additional 15-second intervals, if necessary, until chocolate is melted and mixture is smooth. Cover and refrigerate 1 hour or until solid.

2 Separate biscuits. Scoop out 1 rounded teaspoon chocolate mixture, using melon baller or small teaspoon; place in center of each biscuit. Press dough up and around chocolate; pinch to form a ball. Roll pinched end on work surface to seal dough and flatten ball slightly.

3 Place sugar in shallow dish. Heat oil in small skillet until hot but not smoking. Cook doughnuts in small batches about 30 seconds per side or until golden brown on both sides. Drain on paper towel-lined plate.

4 Roll warm doughnuts in sugar to coat. Serve warm or at room temperature. (Doughnuts are best eaten within a few hours of cooking.)

TIP

For a quicker chocolate filling, use chocolate chips instead of the chocolate-cream mixture. Place 6 to 8 chips in the center of each biscuit; proceed with shaping and cooking doughnuts as directed.

EASY CHEESY

MAC AND CHEESE MINI CUPS

Makes 36 cups

3 tablespoons butter, divided

2 tablespoons all-purpose flour

1 cup milk

1 teaspoon salt

½ teaspoon black pepper

1 cup (4 ounces) shredded sharp Cheddar cheese

1 cup (4 ounces) shredded Muenster cheese

8 ounces elbow macaroni, cooked and drained

⅓ cup panko or plain dry bread crumbs

1 Preheat oven to 400°F. Melt 1 tablespoon butter in large saucepan over medium heat; grease 36 mini (1¾-inch) muffin cups with melted butter.

2 Melt remaining 2 tablespoons butter in same saucepan over medium heat. Whisk in flour; cook and stir 2 minutes. Add milk, salt and pepper; cook and stir 3 minutes or until thickened. Remove from heat; stir in cheeses. Fold in macaroni. Divide mixture evenly among prepared muffin cups; sprinkle with panko.

3 Bake about 25 minutes or until golden brown. Cool in pans 10 minutes; remove carefully using sharp knife.

CHEEJY TOT-CHOJ

Makes 4 servings

½ (32-ounce) package
frozen potato
nuggets

8 ounces uncooked
bacon, chopped

1 cup (4 ounces)
shredded Cheddar
cheese

½ cup sliced green
onions

¼ cup chopped fresh
cilantro

Sour cream and salsa

1 Preheat oven to 450°F. Line large baking sheet with foil.
Spread potato nuggets on prepared baking sheet. Bake
about 20 minutes or until nuggets are golden brown.

2 Meanwhile, cook bacon in medium skillet over medium
heat until crisp, stirring frequently. Remove bacon from
skillet with slotted spoon; drain on paper towels.

3 Push nuggets close together on baking sheet; sprinkle with
cheese. Bake 5 minutes or until cheese is melted. Sprinkle
with green onions, cilantro and bacon. Serve with sour
cream and salsa.

MINI CHEESE DOGS

Makes 32 mini cheese dogs

1 package (16 ounces)
    hot dogs (8 hot dogs)

6 ounces pasteurized
    process cheese
    product

2 packages (16 ounces
    each) jumbo
    homestyle buttermilk
    biscuits (8 biscuits
    per package)

+ ✳ + + ✳ ✳ + ✳ + ✳ ✳ ✳ + + ✳ + ✳

1 Preheat oven to 350°F. Line baking sheet with parchment paper or spray with nonstick cooking spray.

2 Cut each hot dog into four pieces. Cut cheese product into 32 (1×½-inch) pieces.

3 Separate biscuits; cut each biscuit in half. Wrap dough around one piece of hot dog and one piece of cheese; pinch seams to seal. Place seam side up on prepared baking sheet.

4 Bake 15 minutes or until biscuits are golden brown. Serve warm.

QUICK TOMATO & CHEESE PIZZAS

Makes 4 small pizzas

1 teaspoon yellow cornmeal

¾ cup all-purpose flour

¼ cup whole wheat flour

1 teaspoon rapid-rise active dry yeast

½ teaspoon salt

½ cup warm water (120°F)

1 tablespoon olive oil

¼ cup pasta or pizza sauce

12 grape or cherry tomatoes

¼ cup finely diced red pepper

1 cup (4 ounces) shredded mozzarella cheese

4 teaspoons grated Parmesan cheese

1 Preheat oven to 450°F. Spray baking sheet with nonstick cooking spray. Sprinkle with cornmeal.

2 Combine all-purpose flour, whole wheat flour, yeast and salt in medium bowl. Stir in water and oil until soft, sticky dough forms.

3 Turn out dough on lightly floured surface. Knead about 5 minutes or until dough is smooth and elastic, adding additional all-purpose flour as needed to prevent sticking. Shape dough into ball; place bowl over dough and let rest 5 minutes.

4 Divide dough into four equal pieces. Press each piece into 6-inch circle. Place circles on prepared baking sheet.

5 Spread 1 tablespoon sauce over each circle; top with tomatoes and peppers. Sprinkle 1 teaspoon Parmesan cheese and ¼ cup mozzarella over top of each pizza.

6 Bake about 10 minutes or until crusts are golden brown and cheese is melted. Cool slightly; cut into quarters.

CHEESY RAMEN BITES

Makes 2 dozen bites

4 packages (3 ounces each) ramen noodles*

1 can (12 ounces) evaporated milk

2 cups (8 ounces) finely shredded Cheddar cheese

¼ teaspoon salt

¼ teaspoon garlic powder

2 eggs

1 cup panko bread crumbs

Optional dips: honey mustard or ranch dressing

*Use any flavor; discard seasoning packets.

1 Preheat oven to 350°F. Spray 13×9-inch pan with nonstick cooking spray.

2 Cook noodles according to package directions; drain and rinse under cold water to stop cooking. Place in medium bowl; stir in evaporated milk, cheese, salt and garlic powder. Spread noodle mixture evenly in prepared pan. Bake 30 minutes. Remove from oven; cool 10 minutes. Cover and refrigerate in pan at least 4 hours or overnight.

3 Preheat oven to 425°F. Spray large baking sheet with cooking spray. Cut noodle mixture into 24 squares.

4 Beat eggs in small bowl. Pour panko in medium bowl. Working with one at a time, dip noodle squares in eggs, letting excess drip back into bowl. Roll in panko to coat; place on prepared baking sheet.

5 Bake 8 minutes. Turn pieces over; bake 2 minutes. Cool slightly; serve with dip, if desired.

SUPER SIMPLE CHEESY BUBBLE BREAD

Makes 12 servings

2 packages (12 ounces each) refrigerated buttermilk biscuits (10 biscuits per package)

2 tablespoons butter, melted

1½ cups (6 ounces) shredded Italian cheese blend

1 Preheat oven to 350°F. Spray 9×5-inch loaf pan with nonstick cooking spray.

2 Separate biscuits; cut each biscuit into four pieces with scissors. Layer half of biscuit pieces in prepared pan. Drizzle with 1 tablespoon butter; sprinkle with 1 cup cheese. Top with remaining biscuit pieces, 1 tablespoon butter and ½ cup cheese.

3 Bake 25 minutes or until golden brown. Serve warm.

TIP

It's easy to change up the flavors in this simple bread. Try Mexican cheese blend instead of Italian, and add taco seasoning mix and/or hot pepper sauce to the melted butter before drizzling it over the dough. Or, sprinkle ¼ cup chopped ham, salami or crumbled crisp-cooked bacon between the layers of dough.

MOZZARELLA STICKS

Makes 12 sticks

¼ cup all-purpose flour

2 eggs

1 tablespoon water

1 cup plain dry bread crumbs

2 teaspoons Italian seasoning

½ teaspoon salt

½ teaspoon garlic powder

1 package (12 ounces) string cheese (12 sticks)

Vegetable oil for frying

1 cup marinara or pizza sauce, heated

1 Place flour in shallow bowl. Whisk eggs and water in another shallow bowl. Combine bread crumbs, Italian seasoning, salt and garlic powder in third shallow bowl. Place large wire rack over paper towels.

2 Coat each piece of cheese with flour. Dip in egg mixture, letting excess drip back into bowl. Roll in bread crumb mixture to coat. Dip again in egg mixture and roll again in bread crumb mixture. Place on plate; refrigerate until ready to cook.

3 Heat 2 inches of oil in large saucepan over medium-high heat to 350°F; adjust heat to maintain temperature during frying. Cook cheese sticks in batches 1 minute or until golden brown. Drain on prepared wire rack. Serve with warm marinara sauce.

TOASTED RAVIOLI

Makes 20 to 24 ravioli

1 cup all-purpose flour

2 eggs

¼ cup water

1 cup plain dry bread crumbs

1 teaspoon Italian seasoning

¾ teaspoon garlic powder

¼ teaspoon salt

½ cup grated Parmesan cheese

2 tablespoons finely chopped fresh parsley

Vegetable oil for frying

1 package (12 to 16 ounces) meat or cheese ravioli, thawed if frozen

Pasta sauce, heated

1 Place flour in shallow bowl. Whisk eggs and water in another shallow bowl. Combine bread crumbs, Italian seasoning, garlic powder and salt in third shallow bowl. Combine cheese and parsley in large bowl; stir to blend.

2 Heat 2 inches of oil in large saucepan over medium-high heat to 350°F; adjust heat to maintain temperature during frying.

3 Coat ravioli with flour. Dip in egg mixture, letting excess drip back into bowl. Roll in bread crumb mixture to coat.

4 Working in batches, carefully add ravioli to hot oil; cook 1 minute or until golden brown, turning once. Drain on paper towel-lined plate. Add to bowl with cheese mixture; toss to coat. Serve with warm pasta sauce.

CLASSIC MACARONI AND CHEESE

Makes 8 servings

2 cups uncooked elbow macaroni

¼ cup (½ stick) butter

¼ cup all-purpose flour

2½ cups whole milk

1 teaspoon salt

⅛ teaspoon black pepper

4 cups (16 ounces) shredded Colby-Jack cheese

+ ✗ + + ✗ + ✗ + ✗ ✗ ✗ + + ✗ + + ✗ ✗

1 Cook pasta in medium saucepan of salted boiling water according to package directions until al dente. Drain and return to saucepan.

2 Meanwhile, melt butter in large saucepan over medium heat. Add flour; whisk until well blended and bubbly. Slowly add milk, salt and pepper, whisking until blended. Cook and stir until milk begins to bubble. Add cheese, 1 cup at a time; cook and stir until cheese is melted and sauce is smooth.

3 Stir pasta into cheese sauce until blended; cook over low heat until heated through.

CHEESY GARLIC BREAD

Makes 8 to 10 servings

1 loaf (about 16 ounces) Italian bread

½ cup (1 stick) butter, softened

8 cloves garlic, very thinly sliced

¼ cup grated Parmesan cheese

2 cups (8 ounces) shredded mozzarella cheese

✛ ✕ ✛ ✕ ✛ ✕ ✛ ✕ ✛ ✕ ✛ ✕ ✛ ✛ ✕ ✛ ✕

1 Preheat oven to 425°F. Line large baking sheet with foil.

2 Cut bread in half horizontally. Spread cut sides of bread evenly with butter; top with sliced garlic. Sprinkle with Parmesan, then mozzarella. Place on prepared baking sheet.

3 Bake 12 minutes or until cheese is melted and golden brown in spots. Cut bread crosswise into slices. Serve warm.

BARBECUE CHICKEN PIZZA

Makes 4 servings

1 pound refrigerated pizza dough*

6 ounces boneless skinless chicken breasts, cut into strips (about 2×¼ inch)

¼ teaspoon salt

⅛ teaspoon black pepper

1 tablespoon olive oil

6 tablespoons barbecue sauce, divided

⅔ cup shredded mozzarella cheese, divided

½ cup (2 ounces) shredded smoked Gouda cheese, divided

½ small red onion, cut into ⅛-inch slices

2 tablespoons chopped fresh cilantro

*Or use a 12-inch prepared pizza crust.

1 Preheat oven to 450°F. Line baking sheet with parchment paper. Let dough come to room temperature.

2 Season chicken with salt and pepper. Heat oil in large skillet over medium-high heat. Add chicken; cook 5 minutes or just until cooked though, stirring occasionally. Remove chicken to medium bowl. Add 2 tablespoons barbecue sauce; stir to coat.

3 Roll out dough into 12-inch circle on lightly floured surface. Transfer to prepared baking sheet. Spread remaining 4 tablespoons barbecue sauce over dough, leaving ½-inch border. Sprinkle with 2 tablespoons mozzarella and 2 tablespoons Gouda. Top with chicken and onion; sprinkle with remaining cheeses.

4 Bake 12 to 15 minutes or until crust is browned and cheese is bubbly. Sprinkle with cilantro.

WICKED 'WICHES

PROSCIUTTO PROVOLONE SANDWICHES

Makes 4 servings

1 loaf French bread

4 teaspoons whole grain Dijon mustard

4 teaspoons cold butter

2 ounces sliced provolone cheese

4 cups spring greens (4 ounces)

8 ounces prosciutto or other thinly sliced ham

1 Cut bread crosswise into four 6-inch pieces; cut each piece in half horizontally.

2 Spread 1 teaspoon mustard on top halves of bread; spread 1 teaspoon butter on bottom halves. Layer cheese, greens and prosciutto over buttered bread halves. Serve immediately or wrap each sandwich with plastic wrap; refrigerate until ready to serve.

NOTE

Sandwiches may be prepared one day in advance. Wrap with plastic wrap and refrigerate until ready to serve.

SMASHED BACON BURGERS

Makes 4 servings

4 slices bacon, cut in half

1 pound ground beef

Salt and black pepper

4 slices sharp Cheddar or American cheese

4 eggs (optional)

4 brioche rolls or hamburger buns, split

Lettuce leaves

1 Cook bacon in large skillet over medium-high heat until crisp. Drain on paper towel-lined plate. Drain all but 1 tablespoon drippings from skillet.

2 Divide beef into four portions and shape lightly into loose balls. Place in same skillet over medium-high heat. Smash with spatula to flatten into thin patties; sprinkle with salt and pepper. Cook 2 to 3 minutes or until edges and bottoms are browned. Flip burgers; top with cheese. Cook 2 to 3 minutes for medium rare or to desired doneness. Remove to plates.

3 If desired, crack eggs into hot skillet. Cook over medium heat 3 minutes or until whites are opaque and yolks are desired degree of doneness, flipping once, if desired, for over easy. Place lettuce and burgers on rolls; top with eggs and bacon.

TUNA SALAD SANDWICHES

Makes 2 servings

1 can (12 ounces) solid white albacore tuna, drained

1 can (5 ounces) chunk white albacore tuna, drained

¼ cup mayonnaise

1 tablespoon pickle relish

2 teaspoons spicy brown mustard

1 teaspoon lemon juice

½ teaspoon salt

¼ teaspoon black pepper

2 pieces focaccia (about 4×3 inches), split and toasted or 4 slices honey wheat bread

Lettuce, tomato and red onion slices

1 Place tuna in medium bowl; flake with fork. Add mayonnaise, pickle relish, mustard, lemon juice, salt and pepper; mix well.

2 Serve tuna salad on focaccia with lettuce, tomato and onion.

REUBEN SANDWICHES

Makes 2 sandwiches

4 slices rye bread

¼ cup Thousand Island dressing (see Tip)

8 ounces thinly sliced corned beef or pastrami

4 slices (1 ounce each) Swiss cheese

½ cup sauerkraut, well drained

2 tablespoons butter

1 Spread one side of each bread slice with dressing. Top two bread slices with corned beef, cheese, sauerkraut and remaining bread slices.

2 Melt butter in large skillet over medium heat. Add sandwiches; press down with spatula or weigh down with small plate. Cook sandwiches 6 minutes per side or until cheese is melted and bread is lightly browned, pressing down with spatula to crisp bread slightly. Serve immediately.

TIP

For a quick homemade Thousand Island dressing, combine 2 tablespoons mayonnaise, 2 tablespoons sweet pickle relish and 1 tablespoon cocktail sauce in small bowl.

SAUSAGE AND EGG SANDWICHES

Makes 2 sandwiches

2 breakfast sausage patties

3 eggs

Salt and black pepper

2 teaspoons butter

2 slices (about 2 ounces) Cheddar cheese

2 whole wheat English muffins, split and toasted

1 Cook sausage according to package directions.

2 Beat eggs, salt and pepper in small bowl. Melt butter in small skillet over low heat. Pour eggs into skillet; cook and stir just until set.

3 Place cheese on bottom halves of English muffins; top with sausage, scrambled eggs and top halves of English muffins. Serve immediately.

TIP

Sausage breakfast patties may vary in size. If patties are small, use two patties for each sandwich.

MONTE CRISTO SANDWICHES

Makes 4 servings

4 ounces sliced deli turkey

4 slices Swiss cheese

12 thin slices honey wheat or whole wheat bread

4 ounces sliced smoked deli ham

4 slices deli American cheese

2 eggs

¼ cup milk

⅛ teaspoon salt

Pinch of ground nutmeg

2 to 3 tablespoons butter

Powdered sugar

Raspberry preserves

1 Preheat oven to 450°F. Line baking sheet with foil.

2 For each sandwich, layer one quarter of turkey and one slice of Swiss cheese on one bread slice; top with second bread slice, one quarter of ham, one slice of American cheese and third bread slice. Press sandwiches together gently.

3 Beat eggs, milk, salt and nutmeg in shallow dish until blended. Dip both sides of each sandwich briefly in egg mixture, letting excess drip back into dish.

4 Melt 1 tablespoon butter in large nonstick skillet over medium heat. Cook sandwiches in batches 2 to 3 minutes per side or until browned, adding additional butter to skillet as needed. Transfer sandwiches to prepared baking sheet.

5 Bake 5 to 7 minutes or until sandwiches are heated through and cheese is melted. Cut each sandwich in half diagonally; sprinkle lightly with powdered sugar. Serve immediately with raspberry preserves.

MOZZARELLA IN CARROZZA

Makes about 8 servings

2 eggs

⅓ cup milk

¼ teaspoon salt

⅛ teaspoon black pepper

8 slices country Italian bread

8 to 12 fresh basil leaves, torn

8 oil-packed sun-dried tomatoes, drained and cut into strips

6 ounces fresh mozzarella, cut into ¼-inch slices

2 tablespoons olive oil

1 Whisk eggs, milk, salt and pepper in shallow bowl or baking dish until well blended.

2 Place four bread slices on work surface. Top with basil, sun-dried tomatoes, cheese and remaining bread slices.

3 Heat oil in large skillet over medium heat. Dip sandwiches in egg mixture, turning and pressing to coat completely. Add sandwiches to skillet; cook 5 minutes per side or until golden brown. Cut into strips or squares to serve.

TURKEY-BASIL PANINI

Makes 4 servings

8 ounces (half of 1-pound loaf) multigrain or regular Italian bread loaf, cut in half crosswise

3 ounces sliced deli oven-roasted turkey

16 to 20 medium basil leaves

2 ounces (about ⅓ cup) roasted red pepper pieces, larger pieces torn in half

¾ cup (3 ounces) shredded mozzarella cheese

1 to 1½ tablespoons balsamic dressing

1 Slice off top of bread loaf to make a smooth top surface. Hollow out top and bottom halves of bread to make a ½-inch-thick shell.

2 Layer bottom of bread with turkey, basil, red pepper and cheese. Spoon dressing evenly over cut side of top bread slice. Place top bread slice over bottom and press down lightly to adhere.

3 Spray large nonstick skillet with nonstick cooking spray; heat over medium heat. Place sandwich in skillet. Weigh down sandwich with another heavy skillet or stack of plates. Cook sandwich 3 minutes on each side or until golden and cheese is slightly melted. Cut into four pieces.

GRILLED CHEESE KABOBS

Makes 12 servings

8 thick slices whole wheat bread

4 thick slices sharp Cheddar cheese

3 thick slices Monterey Jack or Colby-Jack cheese

2 tablespoons butter, melted

1 Cut each slice of bread and each slice of cheese into 1-inch squares. Make small sandwiches with one square of bread and one square of each type of cheese. Top with second square of bread.

2 Brush four cut sides of sandwiches with melted butter. Stick small wooden skewer or toothpick through each sandwich to hold them together.

3 Heat nonstick grill pan or skillet over medium-high heat. Cook sandwich kabobs 30 seconds on each buttered side until golden and cheese is slightly melted.

STACKED KAISERS WITH SWEET SPICED SPREAD

Makes 4 servings

¼ cup mayonnaise

3 tablespoons yellow mustard

1 tablespoon packed dark brown sugar

1 teaspoon prepared horseradish

⅛ teaspoon ground cinnamon

4 Kaiser rolls, cut in half

6 ounces thinly sliced deli honey-baked ham

6 ounces thinly sliced deli smoked turkey

4 slices Swiss cheese

4 slices American cheese

4 thin slices red onion

8 green bell pepper rings

1 For spread, combine mayonnaise, mustard, sugar, horseradish and cinnamon in small bowl; mix well.

2 Coat cut sides of each roll with about 1 tablespoon spread per side. Arrange ham, turkey, Swiss and American cheeses, onion and bell pepper on the rolls. Top with remaining halves of bread. Press down gently.

STUFFED FOCACCIA SANDWICHES

Makes 4 sandwiches

1 container (about 5 ounces) soft cheese with garlic and herbs

1 (10-inch) round herb or onion focaccia, cut in half horizontally

½ cup thinly sliced red onion

½ cup coarsely chopped pimiento-stuffed green olives, drained

¼ cup sliced mild banana peppers

4 ounces thinly sliced deli hard salami

6 ounces thinly sliced deli oven-roasted turkey

1 package (⅔ ounce) fresh basil, stems removed

1 Spread soft cheese over cut sides of focaccia. Layer bottom half evenly with onion, olives, peppers, salami, turkey and basil. Cover sandwich with top half of focaccia; press down firmly.

2 Cut sandwich into four equal pieces. Serve immediately or wrap individually in plastic wrap and refrigerate until ready to serve.

SPEEDY SIPS

ORANGE WHIP

Makes 2 servings

2 cups ice cubes

1 can (12 ounces) frozen orange juice concentrate with pulp, partially thawed

1 cup milk

¼ cup powdered sugar

½ teaspoon vanilla

1 Combine ice, orange juice concentrate, milk, powdered sugar and vanilla in blender; pulse to break up ice. Blend until smooth.

2 Pour into two glasses; serve immediately.

PEACH FLOAT

Makes 1 serving

2 to 3 scoops vanilla ice cream

4 ounces peach yogurt

2 to 3 ounces cola beverage

Whipped cream or whipped topping

1 Place ice cream in soda or parfait glass; top with yogurt.

2 Pour cola over peach yogurt. Top with whipped cream, if desired. Serve immediately.

ICED CREAMY CHAI

Makes 2 servings

2 spiced chai-flavored tea bags

1 cup boiling water

2 tablespoons sugar

Ice cubes

2 cups cold water

½ cup whipping cream

Ground cinnamon or nutmeg (optional)

1 Steep both tea bags in boiling water for about 4 minutes to brew 1 cup double-strength tea. Remove tea bags; stir in sugar until dissolved. Refrigerate tea until cold.

2 To serve, pour half of cooled tea over ice in each of two tall glasses. Add 1 cup cold water and ¼ cup cream to each glass; stir to mix. Sprinkle with cinnamon, if desired.

PEACH FLOAT

STRAWBERRY MILK SHAKE

Makes 2 servings

2 cups (1 pint) vanilla ice cream

1 cup frozen strawberries, thawed

¼ cup milk

¼ teaspoon vanilla

Pink and red sugar (optional)

1 Combine ice cream, strawberries, milk and vanilla in blender; blend until smooth.

2 Pour into two small glasses. Top with sugar, if desired. Serve immediately.

ESPRESSO SHAKE

Makes 3 servings

1½ cups vanilla ice cream

1 cup whipping cream

1 tablespoon instant espresso powder

½ teaspoon vanilla

1 Combine ice cream, whipping cream, espresso powder and vanilla in blender. Process until smooth.

2 Pour into three tall glasses; serve immediately.

STRAWBERRY MILK SHAKE

CHOCOLATE COOKIES AND CREAM SHAKE

Makes 2 to 4 servings

1¼ cups crushed mini crème-filled cookies (about 3 cups cookies), divided

¼ cup plus 1 tablespoon milk, divided

1¼ cups vanilla ice cream

¼ cup mini semisweet chocolate chips

⅛ teaspoon ground cinnamon

Whipped cream or whipped topping

Mini crème-filled cookies (optional)

1 Combine ½ cup cookie crumbs and 1 tablespoon milk in small bowl; mix with fork until blended. Evenly press mixture into 2 or 4 glasses. Freeze until ready to use.

2 Combine ½ cup cookie crumbs, remaining ¼ cup milk, ice cream, chocolate chips and cinnamon in blender; blend until smooth.

3 Pour chocolate mixture over cookie base in prepared glasses. Garnish with whipped cream, remaining ¼ cup cookie crumbs and mini cookies.

PEANUT BUTTER & JELLY SHAKES

Makes 2 servings

1½ cups vanilla ice cream

¼ cup milk

2 tablespoons creamy peanut butter

6 peanut butter sandwich cookies, coarsely chopped

¼ cup strawberry preserves

1 to 2 teaspoons water

1 Combine ice cream, milk and peanut butter in blender. Process 1 to 2 minutes or until smooth. Add chopped cookies; blend 10 seconds. Pour into two glasses.

2 Place preserves and water in small bowl; stir until smooth. Stir 2 tablespoons preserve mixture into each glass. Serve immediately.

CARIBBEAN DREAM

Makes 2 servings

¾ cup vanilla ice cream

¾ cup pineapple sherbet

¾ cup tropical fruit salad, drained

¼ cup frozen banana-orange juice concentrate

¼ teaspoon rum extract

1 Combine ice cream, sherbet, fruit salad, juice concentrate and rum extract in blender. Blend 1 to 2 minutes or until smooth.

2 Pour into two glasses. Serve immediately.

FROZEN KIDDIE COCKTAIL

Makes 4 servings

1 jar (6 ounces) stemmed maraschino cherries

2 cups lemon sorbet

¼ cup frozen lemonade concentrate

½ cup cold lemon-lime soda

½ cup crushed ice

1 Reserve four cherries for garnish. Place remaining cherries and cherry juice in blender; blend until smooth. Divide cherry purée evenly among four glasses.

2 Place lemon sorbet, lemonade concentrate, soda and ice in blender; blend until smooth. Pour mixture over cherry mixture in glasses; garnish with reserved cherries.

CARIBBEAN DREAM

RASPBERRY SMOOTHIE

Makes 2 servings

1½ cups fresh or frozen raspberries, plus additional for garnish

1 cup plain yogurt

2 tablespoons sugar

1 tablespoon honey

1 cup crushed ice

1 Combine 1½ cups raspberries, yogurt, sugar, honey and ice in blender; blend until smooth.

2 Pour into two glasses. Garnish with additional raspberries.

BLUE FLUFFY SLUSH

Makes 4 servings

1 package (4-serving size) berry blue gelatin mix

1 cup very cold water

2 cups crushed ice

1 jar (7 ounces) marshmallow crème

¼ cup mini marshmallows (optional)

1 Dissolve gelatin in cold water in medium bowl.

2 Combine gelatin mixture, ice and marshmallow crème in blender. Blend 30 seconds to 1 minute or until mixture is slushy.

3 Pour into four tall glasses; garnish with marshmallows.

RASPBERRY SMOOTHIE

CHEESECAKE BROWNIE BLAST

Makes 2 servings

½ cup whipped cream cheese

½ cup half-and-half

2 ice cubes

2 cups (1 pint) vanilla ice cream or frozen yogurt

1 brownie (about 3 ounces), divided

Whipped cream or whipped topping

1 Place cream cheese, half-and-half and ice in blender; blend until combined.

2 Add ice cream; blend until smooth. Break half of brownie into pieces; add to blender container. Pulse 2 to 3 times just until combined.

3 Pour into two glasses. Garnish with whipped cream and remaining half of brownie broken into bits.

SUPERFOOD SMOOTHIE

Makes 1 serving

1½ cups ice cubes

½ banana

½ cup fresh raspberries

½ cup sliced fresh strawberries

½ cup fresh blueberries

½ cup packed torn spinach

Combine ice, banana, raspberries, strawberries, blueberries and spinach in blender; blend until smooth.

NOTE

Fresh or frozen berries can be used to make this recipe. When using frozen fruit, reduce the amount of ice used.

ICY LEMON-LIME SLUSH

Makes 2 servings

4 cups ice cubes

2 cans (12 ounces each) frozen limeade concentrate

1 cup sparkling water

Juice of 1 lemon

Lemon and lime slices

1 Place ice in blender; pulse until crushed. Add frozen limeade concentrate, sparkling water and lemon juice; blend until smooth.

2 Pour into two glasses; garnish with lemon and lime slices.

SUPERFOOD SMOOTHIE

DOUBLE CHOCOLATE MILK SHAKE

Makes 4 servings

3 cups chocolate ice cream

2 cups milk

1 teaspoon vanilla

2 ounces semisweet chocolate, grated

1   Combine ice cream, milk and vanilla in blender; blend about 1 minute or until smooth.

2   Add chocolate; blend just until combined. Pour into four glasses. Serve immediately.

TROPICAL GREEN SHAKE

Makes 2 servings

1 cup ice cubes

1 cup packed stemmed kale

1 cup frozen tropical fruit mix*

½ cup orange juice

2 tablespoons honey or agave nectar

*Tropical fruit mix typically contains pineapple, mango and strawberries along with other fruit.

1   Combine ice, kale, tropical fruit mix, orange juice and honey in blender; blend until smooth.

2   Pour into two glasses.

DOUBLE CHOCOLATE
MILK SHAKE

SHORT & SWEET

LEFTOVER CANDY BARK
Makes about 3 pounds

3 cups chopped leftover chocolate candy

2 packages (12 ounces each) white chocolate chips

1 package (10 ounces) peanut butter chips

○ ○ ○ ○ ○ ○ ○ ○ ○ ○ ○ ○ ○ ○ ○ ○ ○ ○ ○

1 Line 13×9-inch baking pan with parchment paper. Spread candy in prepared baking pan and freeze at least 1 hour.

2 Melt white chocolate and peanut butter chips in large microwavable bowl on HIGH at 45-second intervals, stirring after each interval, until melted and smooth, about 5 minutes total. Towards the end, check every 20 to 30 seconds.

3 Stir in 2½ cups candy and spread evenly in same parchment-lined baking pan; sprinkle with remaining ½ cup candy. Refrigerate about 1 hour or until firm. Break into pieces.

NOTE
For thinner bark, use a sheet pan instead of a 13×9-inch baking pan.

CINNAMON-SUGAR TWISTS

Makes 14 twists

1 package (about 8 ounces) crescent dough sheet

½ cup sugar

1 teaspoon ground cinnamon

1 Heat 2 inches of oil in large saucepan or Dutch oven to 360°F.

2 Meanwhile, unroll dough on work surface. Cut crosswise into 1-inch strips. Roll strips to form thin ropes; fold in half and twist halves together. Combine sugar and cinnamon in baking dish or shallow bowl.

3 Fry twists about 1½ minutes or until golden brown, turning once. Drain on paper towel-lined wire rack 2 minutes; roll in cinnamon-sugar to coat. Serve warm.

DOUGHNUT HOLE FONDUE

Makes 6 servings

¾ cup whipping cream

1 cup bittersweet or semisweet chocolate chips

1 tablespoon butter

½ teaspoon vanilla

12 to 16 doughnut holes

Sliced fresh fruit, such as pineapple, bananas, strawberries, melon and oranges

1 Heat cream in small saucepan until bubbles form around edge. Remove from heat. Add chocolate; let stand 2 minutes or until softened. Add butter and vanilla; whisk until smooth. Keep warm in fondue pot or transfer to serving bowl.

2 Serve with doughnut holes and fruit.

CHOCOLATE PEANUT BUTTER CEREAL TREATS

Makes 2 dozen treats

½ cup peanut butter

⅓ cup semisweet chocolate chips

1 tablespoon butter

5 cups mini marshmallows

6 cups crisp rice cereal

2 packages (4 ounces each) candy-coated peanut butter pieces

1 Line 13×9-inch baking pan with foil; spray with nonstick cooking spray.

2 Combine peanut butter, chocolate chips and butter in large saucepan; heat over low heat until melted, stirring frequently. Add marshmallows; cook and stir 5 minutes or until melted and smooth. Remove from heat. Stir in cereal and one package of candies.

3 Press into prepared pan; press remaining package of candies into top of bars. Cool completely before cutting into bars.

CHOCOLATE-COVERED BACON

Makes 12 slices

12 slices thick-cut bacon

12 wooden skewers (12 inches)

1 cup semisweet chocolate chips

2 tablespoons shortening, divided

1 cup white chocolate chips or butterscotch chips

1 Preheat oven to 400°F. Thread each bacon slice onto wooden skewer. Place on rack in large baking pan. Bake 20 to 25 minutes or until crisp. Cool completely.

2 Combine semisweet chocolate chips and 1 tablespoon shortening in large microwavable bowl. Microwave on HIGH at 30-second intervals until melted and smooth.

3 Combine white chocolate chips and remaining 1 tablespoon shortening in large microwavable bowl. Microwave on HIGH at 30-second intervals until melted and smooth.

4 Drizzle chocolates over each bacon slice. Place on waxed paper-lined baking sheets. Refrigerate until firm. Store in refrigerator.

RAMEN JOY

Makes 2 to 3 dozen pieces

1¼ cups sweetened shredded coconut

1 package (3 ounces) ramen noodles, crushed*

½ cup slivered almonds, coarsely chopped

¾ cup sweetened condensed milk

¾ teaspoon vanilla

¼ teaspoon salt

¾ cup powdered sugar

8 ounces chocolate candy coating

*Use any flavor; discard seasoning packet.

1 Line 13×9-inch baking pan with foil; spray foil with nonstick cooking spray.

2 Heat large skillet over medium heat. Add coconut, noodles and almonds; cook 3 to 5 minutes or until lightly browned, stirring frequently.

3 Whisk condensed milk, vanilla and salt in large bowl until well blended; stir in powdered sugar. Fold in noodle mixture until well blended. Press mixture into prepared pan.

4 Melt candy coating according to package directions; spread evenly over noodle mixture. Freeze 15 minutes or until topping is firm. Remove from pan using foil; cut into bars.

MOCHA MUG CAKE

Makes 1 serving

2 tablespoons whole wheat flour

2 tablespoons sugar

1 tablespoon unsweetened cocoa powder, plus additional for garnish

1½ to 2 teaspoons instant coffee granules

1 egg white

3 tablespoons milk

1 teaspoon vegetable oil

2 teaspoons mini semisweet chocolate chips

Whipped topping or whipped cream

1 Combine flour, sugar, 1 tablespoon cocoa and coffee granules in large ceramic* microwavable mug; mix well. Whisk egg white, milk and oil in small bowl until well blended. Stir into flour mixture until smooth. Fold in chocolate chips.

2 Microwave on HIGH 2 minutes. Let stand 1 to 2 minutes before serving. Top with whipped topping and additional cocoa, if desired.

*Do not use a glass mug; the cake will cook more evenly in ceramic.

COCONUT-CHOW MEIN CHEWS

Makes about 60 chews

1 package (6 ounces)
chow mein noodles

1 cup sweetened flaked
coconut

1 cup semisweet
chocolate chips

1 cup butterscotch chips

1 package (3 ounces)
slivered almonds

1 Preheat oven to 350°F. Arrange noodles and coconut on baking sheet in single layer. Bake 10 minutes or until coconut is lightly browned, stirring once.

2 Melt chocolate and butterscotch chips in top of double boiler over hot (not boiling) water. Remove from heat; stir in almonds, noodles and coconut.

3 Drop mixture by teaspoonfuls onto waxed paper. Let stand until set.

CHOCOLATE PEANUT CRUNCH

Makes about ¾ pound

1 cup milk chocolate
   chips

½ cup semisweet
   chocolate chips

2 tablespoons corn syrup

1 tablespoon shortening

½ cup unsalted roasted
   peanuts

2 teaspoons vanilla

1 Spray 8-inch square baking pan with nonstick cooking
   spray.

2 Melt milk chocolate and semisweet chocolate chips, corn
   syrup and shortening in small heavy saucepan over low
   heat, stirring constantly.

3 Stir in peanuts and vanilla. Spread in prepared pan,
   distributing peanuts evenly. Refrigerate until firm. Break
   into pieces.

SEVEN-LAYER BARS

Makes 2 to 3 dozen bars

½ cup (1 stick) butter, melted

1 teaspoon vanilla

1 cup graham cracker crumbs

1 cup butterscotch chips

1 cup chocolate chips

1 cup sweetened shredded coconut

1 cup nuts

1 can (14 ounces) sweetened condensed milk

1 Preheat oven to 350°F.

2 Pour butter into 13×9-inch baking pan. Add vanilla. Sprinkle cracker crumbs over butter. Layer butterscotch chips over crumbs, followed by chocolate chips, coconut and nuts. Pour condensed milk evenly over all.

3 Bake 25 minutes or until lightly browned. Cool completely in pan on wire rack. Cut into bars.

INDEX